Praise for

stages

"Tramaine Suubi is a visionary love poet, and *stages* makes a singular life feel vaster than the life cycle of a star. In this poetry of dissolution and re-making, of multiplications and expansion, embodied tenderness is a force capable of moving us 'beyond the binary.' As it journeys from personhood to 'people-hood,' Suubi's music shimmers and flashes and connects."

—Mary Szybist, National Book Award winner for *Incarnadine*

"This book presents a young person seeing the world with fresh yet discerning eyes. In *stages*, Suubi is seeking centeredness in an unstable world. From personal journeys throughout and between continents, Suubi asserts the freedom to be themselves, on their own terms. *stages* is a thoughtful, rigorous, and heartfelt collection of a loving voice."

—Tracie Morris, author of *human/nature*

"In a time when 'black will always be the new black,' Tramaine Suubi's newest book, *stages*, crafts new orbits to the oldest questions. As the poems circumnavigate homecomings, desires, and reclamations, the relay baton of sound and syntax passes seamlessly, always ready to hand the reader a line of true substance, a line of unexpected grace, a line of hard-won delight. Suubi insists on playfulness as a site of maturation and love as a protest against multiple erasures. And like celestial bodies, these poems can transfix, predict, and guide one through both dying and newborn light, reminding the reader, 'civility is a performance you savage in your dreams.'"

—Steven Leyva, author of *The Opposite of Cruelty*

"So rarely do we come across a book like *stages*, which mirrors how a day, an hour, a moment—can engage every layer of our being. This collection will dazzle you with swirling musings which authentically ground and unground our desires, histories, and identities."

—Marisa Tirado, author of *Selena Didn't Know Spanish Either*

"The machine of Suubi's work is its clinical eye. Once, we are looking at a gaggle of geese punctuating the gradient sky, meanwhile, elsewhere we are in Kampala, in Suubi's poem, not entirely at ease, aching as the poet aches. Suubi navigates between the outwardly observed and the deeply internal, and the readers are at a crossroads, sometimes witnessing, other times noting the mechanical dance of our small, exiled lives. Both the reader and the poet are intensively complicit in the work. Suubi is a keenly aware poet, and as such, the reader is too. Suubi's sharp, often unblinking, gaze renders each detail with striking precision. What a collection, what a book, what a way to reinvent what African poetry can do, what it will do. A second coming that deserves all the praise for its excellence."

—Adedayo Agarau, author of *The Years of Blood*

stages

stages

poems

tramaine suubi

AMISTAD

An Imprint of HarperCollins*Publishers*

HarperCollins books may be purchased for educational, business, or sales promotional use. For information, please email the Special Markets Department at SPsales@harpercollins.com.

harpercollins.com

FIRST EDITION

Designed by Yvonne Chan

Library of Congress Cataloging-in-Publication Data

Names: Suubi, Tramaine author
Title: Stages : poems / Tramaine Suubi.
Description: First edition. | New York, NY : Amistad, [2026]
Identifiers: LCCN 2025010343 (print) | LCCN 2025010344 (ebook) | ISBN 9780063344952 trade paperback | ISBN 9780063344969 ebook
Subjects: LCGFT: Poetry
Classification: LCC PR9402.9.S883 S73 2026 (print) | LCC PR9402.9.S883 (ebook) | DDC 821/.92—dc23/eng/20250916
LC record available at https://lccn.loc.gov/2025010343
LC ebook record available at https://lccn.loc.gov/20

Printed in the United States of America

25 26 27 28 29 LBC 5 4 3 2 1

to my patu,
my favorite reader

I insist upon my right to be multiple . . .
Even more so, I insist upon
The recognition of my multiplicity . . .
I really do insist that others recognize my inherent multiplicity
What I no longer do is take pains to explain it or defend it
That is an exhausting, repetitive, and draining project
To constantly explain and defend one's multiplicity
So I've reached a point where
I am aware of my inherent multiplicity
And anyone wishing to meaningfully engage with me or my work
Must be too . . .
—Taiye Selasi, *græ by Moses Sumney*

stages

yellow dwarf

makeshift

when i was four
i wore a creamy amber skirt
to every spectacular event
in my preschool fantasies
outgrew it when i was six
but i clung on then moved
it from my waist to my temple
swished in the wet season
flapped in the dry
transfigured myself majik
you could not tell me anything
in those honeyed waves
was far too busy dancing down
my dark continent from
nandi to makeda to nzinga
the pale billboards of lightening
cream did not sway my baobab skin
every scab was a garnet unto me
caught neatly on my peach waves
never loved a piece of fabric so
purely, keep the memories
tucked in lightning streaks
at my velvet hips

sunkissed

seaglass grazes my toes
stranded kelp graces my wrists
i feel an ease being teased out of me
the caking shore recedes further
before it rushes back, giddy
with foam at the crest. i trough
deeper in the brine & commune
with abandoned shells. in comes
another swell just in time to pop
me up again. brushes of exhaust
decorate a cerulean sky before a bored sun
wades toward a pinked horizon. upon
further inspection, blackberry bushes huddle
near & spotted dunes climb far. in theory
i am returning home, back to my original form
of bluing greens. in reality, the tossing
renders me free, an animal at the mercy
of an unknowable sea

feathered

upon meditating on an unkindness of ravens
i give in to a murder of crows then slowly fade
to a shimmer of hummingbirds. i am drawn back
to earth by a parliament of owls which soon disperse
to who knows where. a convocation of eagles feels
too formal, but morphs to pinpricks as they distance
& death spiral below. a wake of buzzards is at the ready
but steady goes a host of sparrows, unflappable
as they twine with a gulp of swallows. as the sun bids me
well, a gaggle of geese punctuate the gradient sky
my sweetened dreams of tropics are dressed
in a flamboyance of flamingos, yet they fly far
too soon, leaving me to bathe in an oranged morning
that is orchestrated by a drumming of woodpeckers
so i rise in elation as a murmuration of starlings swoop
me into the heavenly throng, just in time for us
all to become one. a flock for the ages

body me water

river me still
ocean me deep
lake me quiet
sea me through
brook me gentle
creek me tender
spring me high
bay me low
gulf me whole
stream me loose
pool me near
pond me far

sink tings

jojoba oil for low porosity edges
upside down olive oil creme w/ castor oil
for extra strength
argan oil buffers the brittle strands
tea tree oil is a teeny weeny essential
aloe only for softnin & coolin
charcoal faces the worst but grins
coconut oil overlaps with teeth, skin & coils
down your throat
sores & stones need peroxide
but saltwater is the everycure
silicone gone, sulfates no more
parabens plucked out
& fuck the alcohol

nostalgia

release
all the bull
& the shit. making
the best mistakes
of this one life, smoked
screens show it all. such
decadence in wildly
heated choices, the joyful
sorrows of this decade. the stale
nights, the rotten days
they all absorb & refract
the muchness of this roaring
decade. the yearning lances
through us all

third avenue

jazz drips on the corner
pedestrians flash
lights & conversation halts

when the big band begins
to color the air
as we patter in time to the rain & slink

into a big city summer, slower
we rock gently, kiss hardly & speak
us with soft clarity

kampala

twenty-two hours of sleep for a whole week
trekking back home but this time not the mountain
not the gorillas. gold entrances & exits do not soften
the char of ochre, the pool of dust, flashing sounds meet bright voices

light the expressway
every word feels hot, urgent
when steeped in the dry season, the great lake anchors me
still my elephant heart is prone to wander, get trapped in the roundabout

matatus are slick & boda bodas never slow
marvel at the hawkers & squawk at the hail
ginger like beard, currant like drink, rusty like path
pack dark & travel heavy to keep from backsliding, mind the teeth

sharpen the smile, all the while the horizon aches
to kiss you again, make love with the call to prayer
glimpse the scarlet blush of sunrise & lick fene off the noon-drunk skin
catch the crimson glance of sunset & make peace with hallowed rain of hima

sit with all you want to but never give to the nile
watch breathlessly as nsenene silver a sagging city sky

first word

also my favorite word: tunda
a moniker for the best fruit juice bantu can conjure
started babbling majik before my first solar return
my most common compliment is sweet—like tunda
golden child of passion fruit & sugar cane
spilling pulp on my last school uniform
yellow was our color

picking up where gwendolyn leaves off in spring to burst
into summer. libations for the suicidal sleep laced
with beatitudes, fruit flush with bountiful seeds
whole waters filling the budding grove in my belly
aches betray petty lies that i tell for fun
funny how i am the best liar i know
knowing only matters
if you know what you do not
know

indian summer

i shit talk the stocks
with cicadas & crickets
stake my lot on all i got

in between, i suckle the honey
bird the humming, fire the fly
to top it off, i hop the grass
& rub twin freckles in my eye

snap back forlorn, baby fat intact
love dripping from the handles
thunder taut my thighs

sunnet

sundrunk
& sunk in
teeth, hot to the skin
wafting on an icy breeze
seizing all coherence start
postponing wallows into
amber daisies of unease
bobbing on the crest
as the cacophony swells & snatches
of gossip pierce through the wings
languid equinox melts into the dandelion
drains all your fixations & dazzles you silly
soak in chantilly but gnaw the lace of your cheek
civility is a performance you savage in your dreams

stone

fruit of my labor
savor me in the ripe sun
run back to the present
cast me in plums
hums in between a bite of peaches
leeches my bones dry & drops eaves
leaves me laced in secrets
frets until i pass the pit in my belly
jelly knees wobble at the sight of you
true to the murmur of my heart
art drips off my fingertips
chips away at the apricot
got caught doing my best
lest you think otherwise
size me up & palm the mango
tango with my fears til they subside
hide them where i cannot feel
steel me for the decision
envision me on the lake with avocado
bravado forsaken as we embrace
trace the skin to skin as i bare

pearls

suck in sleep in tiny swallows
ignoring the birds crashing
into the lofty window, i swallow
all the women i have never loved
through a refracted lens, i crash
into myself when i most expect it
but it takes a big sulk to be the baby
i cannot be anymore, more is the new black
& i will not take that back, cease the night
despite my waning delight, i wake alight
in a pool of bruleéd sunrise
size, as it turns out, does matter
mastery is a great white lie, here
is my empirical evidence, density will vary
but i am never precise
in the guessing game, names
do not depower me anymore

triangulation

these days my mind
is wary of my body, my spirit wary
of my mind. my mind watches
my body, intently, all patient-like
glides in neutral just to see
which way my body steers
when no one is driving. my spirit
disembodied, floats astride my flesh
not quite sure how to land
in my skin, not sure where my mind
sits with my body too. a discor(d)ance
of sorts. a grafted orchestra. an estranged
symphony, perhaps. hope we return
to a holey trinity, somehow

outliving

we carry our dead with us
haul them up & about in our
boneless spirits, in our fractal
minds, pieces of their laughter
scraps of their tears, traces
of their sorrowful joys, dear yet near
tattoo them on our ears, brand them
on our tongues, wail their deathdays
& sob their birthdays. wallow about
in the meanest time, we carry
our dead within us, caressed
through our memories, buoyed
by our imaginations, we await
the moment we return
our cheek upon their cheek
love beyond love

whirlpool

bring me the drink of the gods
        run me through the potential of loss

open the silt for your pleasure
        at your leisure renew the filter

so the sinew can be loosed
        choose how waves crash

capsize my hippocampus before the pale
        demon breaks ground in dry blood

red giant

idle

we make the rarities our gods
& put our mediocre on display
while anchored to said gods, we talk
along the lines we chalk up for fun

we make the schtick our majik
& watch watches tick faster
than our breath of a life line
so fragile we are, even more so
than the cinched waste of the hourglass

we make good on our penchant for camp
disband the orderlies at random
dance with disaster for the frills of it
neverminding how often we stall in the milieu

we make light of our death march
to the sea & manufacture tranquility
sold to the loneliest bidder, every single time
is it not sublime, how cheap dreams can be
sipped through a straw

uptick

we are wrapping up as the protest marches
past our window. the third story blinds barely mask
the shrill rage of call & response, the swell
is coming. the march, relentless. the cry rings higher
crescendos before we finish. i think back
to the black trans lives matter march in pigtown
how we lay on the street, how we lie in these sheets
while the lye is shit & ruins my tar strands, baby

the only time i am stopped by a baltimore cop, i take
a hard left in the wrong lane & my diaphragm
winds so tight, all i can squeak out is sorry
to this light skinned cop who looks so
sorry for me. i suppose pity works in lieu of pretty
privilege, so i peel out without a fine
my watered eyes stay dammed until a little black boy
makes silly faces in a window & blows me a kiss

cost to coast

portland is my fever dream of choice
so i hop on the flight of fancy
off to pacific specifics

the northwest stains ruddy in my memory, lanes
swerve, give way to mountain glories
a sort of piney haven

portland beckons a tram to maine & the locals
offer me atlantic balms, palm the leftover
brine after whale watching past bedtime

the northeast keeps me grounding & abandoning
mining the amerikkkan nightmare as it creaks
crumbling at the closures

grace african braiding salon

the braiders are adorned in crisp contours & popping purples / trade updates in fast french & debate the length of my hair / their hair is smoother than my afrikan accent / but i need the hidden discount so i trudge on / privately consider the pink hair for sale in the corner / the women are venting about bouncing checks / their frustration rings louder than their praise music / i miss my favorite housegirl / wonder if she chose to stay behind because she saw through the smokescreens of amerikkka / next time i could ask for the pink braids / all the way down to my hips / my back curls as the first woman asks me if i am igbo / i laugh them off as two other tongues get stuck in my throat / their gossip bubbles up / i found out my test was a false positive / fantasize about running in pink braids / cotton candy cascading down my back / the second woman calls her sister & tells her to soak the dry fish outside / i notice the rain / maybe the pink braids will finally make me the main character of my own story / my birthday is in five days but i am too exhausted to serve my life expectancy / maybe God will give me parole if i keep up the good behavior / i miss my favorite braider / wonder if her husband stopped drinking other women without wiping off the scent / the woman next to me gets out of her chair / cancels her appointment / i drown in secondhand embarrassment / the woman is dragged in three languages until noon / i close my book / imagine wearing pink braids to the wedding in two months / the third woman jabs at my book / asks why the cover shows a woman spreading her legs / i bite back every impulse / to apologize / pretend not to hear her question / she clicks her tongue at me & returns to their gossip / i clench hard when the first woman tightens my braid / tilts my head for the ninety-ninth time / i should have taken a thousand milligrams of ibuprofen / my growth is getting difficult / i miss my favorite auntie / wonder if she still mixes ungodly wealth with prosperity gospel / i was raised by ruthless women / who hide two machetes between their teeth / the tv blinks twice / switches to nollywood / the female lead suffers endlessly / no one has hugged me in eight days / my skin has never felt thinner / i notice the sun / my ends are finally singed / finger the pynk hair one last time / use the hidden discount / cash only

old habits

you are an undying skeptic
times stay hectic so you mind your own
watch, but the brain is prone to skip records
regardless, memory pays no attention
the price is too steep, so déjà vu grows
familiar. as you stir the tea, tap twice
on the teacup in hopes of drifting out
of a sunken place. reversing curses takes
work & often will not soften the root
of the banal. dwell then. despite
what the sages & gurus contend
ruminate back here, soak your buds
in a past that tastes of ember
rekindle the notes, negotiate the rate
as you recede downhill. bathe in the mud
wade in the valley, swap songs with the shadow
sides. compromise in the end & be content
with meeting halfway, though you do not
love with half of the heart. forget this not
the times will always tell on you

sapphy

after she   breaks   out of my heart
i become siren
& mealpiece my revenge
punish anyone
who dares to love me
after her. steal her lines
& stuff them
down my throat
until my cruel tastes just
like her. wager pride
against the fear
of rejection then   win   every single dime

baker miller pink

color me a shade removed from insanity
give or take about fifteen minutes of small talk
i will antacid you into tranquility
then at the quarter hour
watch you unravel from the inside out
in a drunk tank hallucination that will
sideways tilt your world leaving you
stranded in some uncanny valley of your own
creation, find time to speed up & itch
at the growing agitation in your skull
but remember that first fourth of serenity? claw aimlessly
through marzipan & realize you will never bloom
bubblegum like you were promised & flummoxed
or is it i or is it we will settle for the metal & cotton
candy cage of baker miller pink

sheet cake

praise be
for such
excess. gratitude
for the glutton's greed
for now, you
are not
the sinner
in this moment, you
are pure
sugar genes

silky satin

no one knows why we are
thin lines, pink clouds, jam wine
scarlet skirt, iridescent irises

big sky country yellows your layers
the baby grand honeys your buttered words
entranced & shaken, but not mistaken

drunk on my frothy blues
nothing can cover the crooning in us
come, darling, drink my cooling azure

solarpowered

i step off the mothership
disembark
my sun sign is muted
in the distant future
so i slow my pace
as i gauge this new terrain
the abundance of my home
planet is in ruins
but i trudge on
with our rescue mission
pause to meditate
on the affection of my kisser
my stolen sapphire
& watch my eyes mist her

mine

body
wars against itself
every day
an unwitting hazard
to my self
an implosion in progress
how do you neutralize
the enemy
you cannot
hear, see, smell, taste, touch
how do you neutralize
the self

gunning

we all got triggers
nurse mine
three times a day
make sure i stay
unloaded
click them
back when, ever, i
catch astray
the kick is merciless
but i shoulder through
regardless of the ricochet

physically

gravity is working
on me so i gravitate
towards a better velocity
& finetune energies

forces remain pretty neutral
with my attitude, so i cruise
to my ideal latitude

suspending my belief, i meditate
on the heisenberg principle then
tussle with the fallacy of choice

hope stunningly intact, i wade
through fallow ground & dream
of mustard seeds for a greener spring

life travels at the speed of sound, death
travels at the speed of light, i hear
your laughter best after i see you
in the casket

jane roe

makes me feel a pregnant numbness
& i tell my favorite therapist. like hollowing
my throat to scream but there are no decibels
to be found. the antidepressants are doing their job too
well so i have not cried in four days even
though it is cancer season. when i do feel peace
in this timeline, it is only on airplanes
a kind of perfect purgatory. no responsibilities
no identities, just me & mazes of patchwork
tend to shell out extra for the window seat
even though my account is perpetually broke
& dodging these overdraft fees wears on me
the racket is too ricket
for my exponentially nervous system but i dream
of piloting. that is my mother's dream job
she still dreams of labor, courtesy of the ecclesiastes
she settles for accounting instead
second choices do not taste as sweet as second chances
pity. the baby in the window seat babbles in a language
only we can silly. the mother sighs her thanks to me

calamity

the audacity of living, the sheer
fuckery of being alive & wet
in this helter-skelter universe

what a society
a shock of blood to the sacral
no one knows anything, yet

the parade hums on, the clowns
chuckle incessantly
in threes

how do we remain porous
make sure that the violence of waking up
to another day is fresh in our lagging bones

i caress the scars
but forget to dress the wound
& now everything is muddied

soft rocks keep me company
in my socks on this soggy
morning & i compose

a borrowed harmony
for the disquieting
afternoon

wind chimes across the lakeshore
makes me content to wander
the geography of her skin

when autumn leaves me behind
remember this september, how we keep it
together while we weep in copper & gold

i crawl down my throat, pull the thing up
air out the wound in a crisp flutter
& flush all the clotting lies

god, savior & hero reconvene
thank heavens for my trinity complex
how else would i dance through the cacophany

clustercuss

so i retrograde with mercury
throw all my tantrums at once
& eclipse right by venus
barely clipped at the apogee
mars topples in time for kinship
turned to rust, as it must
with the witness of jupiter's eye
so i call upon my saturn return
& ponder on the bright side
of over one hundred moons
after the noon, as i shuffle
through slate lakes of jilted neptune
& frozen oceans of tilted uranus
to round out the trip, i scheme
in the corner with pluto on
how to end the untelevised
revolution with the biggest of bangs

fazed

yet my resting bitch face does not perform
on command, does not respond
to cat-calling & cat-fighting
& rogue fingers on my hair & my skin & my

n
a
i
l

unlocking my first defense: freeze
firing blank faces at the leers of old men,
of white men, of young men, of black men
or, honestly

b
o
y
s

how revealing that my bitch only barks
when defending her beloveds, going hellhound
on your ass for making my baby sister cry, twice
if you still dare to bring her down

a
g
a
i
n

yet queer, really, that my bark is infinitely worse
than my bite, a savaged unholy, but both
will eviscerate you if given a reason
any reason to

ziggurat

tunnel my bowels
temple me holy
soften me dark moss
line me with gold
embalm me alive, mark
my shrieks in brick for posterity
punish me for telling truth too well
later, i resurrect, disappointedly
in the perfect body of a pallid woman
lost on safari. witch me well with this
shiny vessel, as i apocalypse your new world

nakba

their blue sunbirds steel themselves
iron-sharpened iron clashing, under fire

half their yellow maqluba blasting west
the other half catapulting east, under fire

adorning their corpses in their red poppies
tell us where they have not been, under fire

giving for giving's sake, unforgotten
recalling an ambered hope, under fire

how they run on fumes, heart first
fist unfurled, they spur on, under fire

beloved, wane one more crescent here
as they drink the bleached night, under fire

cruel, truly, that the only way out
is through, raging uncaged, under fire

white dwarf

barre

grand jeté jolts my achilles heel
        the set sails forth before my lies
lose my proportions
        & tilts as the world turns askew
grasp loosens & resigns
        farther, forgive me, for i cannot mend
the crack, gut the arrow
        so hollow, i crawl into my self
tidy a space for my sallow & throw
        a pity party for two, sans the prima
who fades, deeper into yesteryear
        she sees the fall coming but does not
have the foresight to warn me, still
        shadows wax while spirits wane

pending

while waiting
for the results, i get
two pothos plants, then
i shave my head
for the third time, afterwards
i pierce my other ear, near
a lone freckle. i sign
up for yoga & pilates while
i exchange four dozen books
for bookstore credit. i order fifty
more books online anyway. i beat
over one thousand levels of a game
but the organic greens wilt again
i lose myself in the frozen foods
the protest marches on, the boycott
rides steady & none of the emails find me
well. both of the home teams play off & lose
to the slurs. my skin itches from the fasting
so i tighten my killswitch. against orders
wean myself off the medications
& reorder my moods. decline
job offers for the hell of it yet
accept two more diagnoses
the smile does remain
dimpled, but the cold cuts
through regardless. the soy
candles continue to burn, incensed
on my behalf, the only salve
still cooling

after hours

she says at least i am self aware, remarkably so
but i still choose the second skin
she asks why i elect for the chasm
for the polite distance when
grace—in lieu of praise—can be abundant, yet
the can is a gamble. the currency of social interactions
runs me dry, cuts me bitter, hence the fort
every animal must evolve & build a protective layer
who am i to seek exception
for me, posture does the talking & switching
codes is a secret weapon. shame
me all you want, wonder at the layers
of fortification. leave me to cocoon
still licking wounds that have yet to see the light

kitchen sink

the life of a knife
splice the rice
& watch it sticky your demise

fluff is pretty tough
squish the fish
& hear it mush your delight

soup for the group
swish the dish
& smell it tinge your descent

stream of conscientiousness

tick tocking makes me crave the femme & the masc
but who has time for this panic, more than we do
after all we do, for their convenience, for no recompense
foam abounds as i meander down the aisle with no expiration
someone cleans up next door before a new soul fills the vacancy
my comfort film is fantastic but that does not change the fact
that beyoncé is my comfort capitalist despite leaving
the child of destiny for bigger & better disappointments
let me order a venti chai latte, i mean a grande iced matcha
big skincare does not actually care about men, no one does
not even men or menses or the most righteous meninists
masochism is my raisin d'être in this sundown town
fuck, it feels good to stop pretending to care about caring

unbirding: one

heart flutters awake
dreamland slips past
the horizon
blinded window marks
three feathers lingering
in memorial
looking down would only prove
an injured truth, expose a muted death
of a gray bird on this spring morning
how quickly a sound is forgotten
unmoved, the stained glass

unbirding: two

my baby blue hatchback is no match for the snap
attack of roadkill, the ruched plumage of an end
anticlimactic does not hack the half of it
the sky remains offensively bright
the sun beams on, empty of eulogy
a curse upon the tyranny of hurry
a groaning for the impact of metal
to feather to metal again
strangely, there is no body
in sight, no thing to bury
so i scurry onward
to my appointment
& release only a tear
in the mourn

yule

in some near
path tread lightly & enter a new dimension
summon the whole spectrum
of me & set the table for thirteen
my last supper fills me with hunger & ashes
note the tired christmas tree, flash
back to the pastel eggs & three days feels too short
to be dead
need far more time to rest, to grieve my tedious life
sacrifice should suffice but i am a reluctant pilgrim
did not ask to be born
barely stop short of asking to die
every floorboard in this house has something
to say, my mother always has something to say
i want desperately to offer resolution but

portrait of my father

king james & holman warned
me about gaslighting
before i ever knew
what it was
as a peacemaker on the enneagram
my father should know better
but then again he still rosies
the poverty of his childhood
& the tectonic grandfather i never met
with more wives than banana trees
he calls for peace, peace, when there is no peace
longs for simpler times & i cry when i remember
how my grandfather left his daughters out of his will
          father quietly gave his sisters his slice of the land
he says i burn too angry, names me wildfire & signs me up
for letters from the marines when i turn sixteen
tells me i need to burn in a straight line
a poet once told me a woman matures when she stops
being a daddy's girl & starts listening to the wound in her mother's
nagging & fussing, the wound, carved by her father
dutifully salted by my father
shapes the cycles & traumas
            festering & unremembering

unfolding

today i try
on my dad's suits

shake loose memories
that roll out too, by twos

hug me in neat pleats & rolls
but they give me room to breathe

earth tones flush against primary colors
dusty in the corner, his sturdy trust me blue

they are well worn but i wear them well
comfort my hurting when no one else does

each suit is set with a stutter in a handkerchief
a proper gentleman armed with the queen's english

he once mused, my first day of school was the happiest
day of his life . . . i am still looking for that suit

his brother's last supper
second easter in kampala

third proposal to my mum
fourth time as the best man

business school outside london
sixth snow, solo, in new york city

seventh gig as a wedding emcee
christmas family reunion in houston

another blood clot struck above paris
10,000 five-stars after ten years as a driver

his mother's fatal stroke on april fools' day
the 99th job interview in this godforsaken country

we do not talk about charlie

uncle, here, is the good kind of funny, a gentle one even
until the virus positively smears him. the only salvation
offered at this time in a burgeoning neocolonial capital
is self-flagellation. a public self-denial, forced swallowing
of the Spirit. he renounces all his lovers, irrespective
of gender & his benders. compares them to the bottle
a palatable sin of the flesh. yes, little else to do but delay
the decay & fit him for a stiff suit from the cheap fashion
district, while his mother thanks Almighty that she will bury
her son proper. nearing the end, he pens silent elegies for all
the selves he kills for a bought dignity. yet, in a time when
deficient immunities beget acquired syndromes, beget regret
he returns to his gentleness that still shrouds him in name
as my father waters his perennials on the anniversaries

bruv

one hundred & thirty-six minutes cease to exist
in the space of a multidimensional phone
call. hearing everything in the hall
humming along as he spells out the mirror
questing life more fervently than a saint
he chuckles low
    wishes he could bar higher
    wants to stick the landing
but needs the notes

babyface adorned in midnight skin
eyes lower than most, boasts honestly
takes stock before the trickshot
shuffles through the world in bass
clef, chin high to the sky

the kid is cooler than nitro
treads water lightly but earthquakes
the soundwaves. his favorite
color channels orange
& trips red in the dead of morning
sweet talks his way out on short notice
his guard is back up, until the wall
of butterflies bursts into a sham
    rustling cocoons
cause after all, we know what happens
to sunkissed boys with waxy wings

cracks

in a dream, my mother slaps me, hard
sends my mind spinning
as my memories crash, my mother brakes
hard, conjures the seams
the gauzy curtains offer translucent kisses
upon the welts, undetectable to my mother
the gauzy curtains veil my father, at the kitchen
table, ever perpendicular to my mother's faults, the hurt
lingers, traces the engorged silence on translucent rays
my mother dreams, hard, spinning me on her back
into a transparent past, curtained by an embittered maturity
the superfluous words of a mere child taken so seriously
that the slap fades into gauzy memory but remains
welted into a most fevered dream

birth rights

firstborn is a predictably precarious
spot on the board. i am still wire
in my frame, oddly comfortable
onstage. the elders elect me to play
the first song at the dirge
they overestimate me when
i least expect it

as a first daughter of a first daughter
imagine my mother at seventy-three
my child in her rearview mirror
a lopsided miracle of my own making
let us undo thin braids in her thinner hair
a trembling of fear with nonsense
in the undercurrent, she questions me
with her answers: an albatross
with no red herring, a tide sans the rip
so in love with another's lover. unmapped
in my grandeur & painstaking, unstoried
again by my ancestors & unrecalled
by my descendants, invisible ink marks
the spot, bangles clashing with calabash
clanging, why ask why not, when the myth
remains recycled. God's right, i am holey
whether lots are cast or not

to my first daughter i say
offspring bubble up. they leap before i
can look for set traps. the weight
is not worth its wait in gold. just coin my name
before my mother names me by instinct
balming will never be enough. i run
my finger up my family, lined with guilted secrets
& commit miracles like the crime they ought to be

changeling

how do i tell my mother
that she gave birth to a hurricane
part shapeshifter & part indigo child
an othered thing
                                        at any given moment
i am bending the rain, faithfully. wish
my reckless skinfolk knew my power
to cleanse in mere seconds

they warn, the child who is not embraced
by the village will burn
it down to feel its warmth. well
consider me a second coming
undaughtered water
                                        giver & taker of life
capable of making each one of them
wish they were drowning
in the lake of fire instead

black
dwarf

ideation

imagine that i wade & wade & wade
waist deeper into the center
spiral farther down & farther out
to the innermost of it all. consider which love
would be the first to go go go, brow
furrowed, as i burrow past
this flimsy covalent bondage. could be
that the vessels pop first, or my wondering eyes
in happy surrender. perhaps bones would embrace
the crush, give in to the rush of blues. floating lower
& lower still, maybe my internal drums burst in sync. left
only with my sensitive taste & touch, my skin breaks
into song. finally color matched & swaddled
in the warmest darks. homebound, let us say i tease
out a last push, inhale the ending. then, a light, a sort
of rude wakening. wrenched ashore, i blink off kilter
unspiraled & heavy with sleep. farther than ever from my center

poise

all my pills spread out
across the apartment
window sills cannot balance them
some fancy the orange bottle
others rest on the swedish bookcase
some are lost under my bright white fridge
more recently they are packaged
sweetly in my black mirror. damn
these perfect pills for keeping me alive
but barely. awake but sleepy, happy but rarely
whether popped, sucked, crunched, gnawed
by my wonderless smile, they grant me
an unwanted gift, an elongated stay, perhaps
a delay of everyone's inevitable flight. but fighting
is futile so i make like the good girl
i am domesticated to be. my expensive training
will not go to waste, like my will, so i still
the theatrics. yet another girl, interrupted

tether

self, help
me. steer we clear
guide us true, through
all the lingered repressions
caught within, as compulsive
obsessions curl up stuck
in my gut. unordered, i bite
down, deep in these bones, know
there is no need to cast doubt
when i will forget me. knot
in belly corresponds to truth telling
which spells bubbling trouble
for my ever elusive double

affixed

i wish to un-me, un-be
on this rock that dis-loves
every tilted second of my existence

i wish to pre-forget, pre-forfeit
the blessing of being broken
by dead-end roads with drop-offs

ablution

bury me in mami wata
scrub through the residue
soak me in the froth of yesteryear
tell me all things i become
in my shallow swim towards telos
snake past my sins, preserved
in each cherry picking
through parts of me. drupes undress
aplenty, but they are pitted against me
since i lack a certain genus
pedal the remnants of my heart chambers
empty them, sound by sound
what sits still in the silt is but
a screen, a cover for the other window
to my quartered soul

heard

ciphers whisper sweet bitters
back between memory & molar
the aftertaste, tinged
an afterthought, a lukewarm balm

in gilead, the physician is still missing
a false god stumbles in, immediately found
wanting, he offers empty homilies
drunk on his effervescence

we are inevitable. we bear reluctant witness
to this anthropocene birthed from our holocene
so hyphenated we are, so prefixed
in the self, we remain

hot air

jeremiah declares God damn amerikkka
& i holler in time to his lamentations
prophet weeping from the pulpit in vain
knowing he shares cassandra's curse
& stolen covenant, yet he will not
concede to apathy. ah but what does
a chicago pastor on the south side
have to do with troy & jericho
woe unto the mighty
city that is thought impenetrable
under the siege of 77 trumpets or 1 hollow horse
or 365 kilos of crack. shallow elegies for empires built
on guns & germs & steel
getting high on their very own supply

inheritance

my savaged country tis of thee
the rugged cross & the lynching tree

on capitol hill, three black bodies hung
as marsha weeps for trans women unsung

red tape runs through our plastic blood
overflowing past the gulf's oily flood

we dance on millions of indigenous graves
& sing off-key for camouflaged braves

paint the smoggy skies once more
with profit, stock & emissions galore

funding genocide, with no means, to no end
myrrh is an ever-present friend

my ailin loves

flint was the first black city to fall
she still carry lead, as the feds stall

jackson fell flat, in the water war
he still talk tough, while pumping no more

baltimore tripped in line at the dirge
she still aim high, while trying to purge

port-au-prince still drownin in shallows
his vodou priestess slips through gallows

cairo up in alms as the nile flees
she still cough dry, unheard in her pleas

nairobi just limps different these days
he shrivelin up in real strange ways

cape town been flogged in the harsh daylight
her soft keenin answers every night

in memory of those who chose the other sea

i moor my self on these ssese islands, rather than wait
for my soul to sop while transoceanic, with raw ankles

lake nalubaale buoys me as i lead
a revolt against you for daring to baptize

my obsidian skin in sin, to soak my largest organ
in your guilt, i say no more

no longer will i pacify your shame, your desperate claws
at absolution. take back your projections & pathetic fallacy

feed those tears to the ancient crocodiles of our nile
unblink the noble savage & uncuff the magical

negro, to take back our final hour. foreign iron
evaporates from our wrists & clasping shaky hands

in reverence, we, my sisters & me, submerge
return to our all-forgiving mother, the sea

the modern white man's burden

perfuming the corpse is wretched
work, but as necessary as a lesser
evil. as with most higher callings
one must divorce their heart
from their head for maximum
efficiency. the corpse bloats
so one must be vigilant in this
great work. use a citrus base
in the summers, turn
to alpine notes in the winters. waft floral notes
in spring, fade to a spiced base in fall. dead
of night is the optimal time of day
for a full coating. the youth must not see
this precious toil & the elderly must not
be reminded. replace the rotted teeth with the enslaved
just like our first forefather. embalm only the palatable
parts & harvest the real treasures, in the name
of our science, but always keep the corpse
in plains, cite the need for a monument, for art. when it rains
let the clouds offer you respite. when it snows, you may retreat
to the heat. punish all who attempt
a formal burial, a dignified homegoing. call them
revisionist, while you rewrite the obituary. drench them
in blood while the corpse reeks of heaven. mock all
who cry, "corpse" & deny its every existence. always
use the pronoun, "it." sneers will follow, jeers will rise
with the temperature, just tender the corpse
in the very best the french can concoct. the belge oblige
by offering stolen chocolate to sell
to nauseated passerbys. these two have the most experience

in this macabre art, so it is best to borrow
their style. carry on with the seasons, dress the corpse
accordingly, host competitions for the best designers, cycle
through the finest rouge, the richest oils. in time, the public
grows attached to the corpse, you receive
volunteers, donations even. they grow so
attached they do not notice
it anymore than the fish
notice the warming waters

courses

unfurling this fraying map
i trace the river up the east
coast, linger at the scar of changing
topography on each bank. the map is up
side down & i cannot reorient
a stubborn current older than any border
on this bastardized cartography. i return
to my spine to feel the echoing
river. the charted course winding
up my back, as pockmarked as the delta. veering
off course, there floats a reminder
of babies in baskets & legends
of godly happenings. rife with ache
the white caps run rapid & swallow
all hesitation. nations squabble over dams
but mother river runs on, unblinking. in
thinking of counter moves, i unspool
my own liquidity & flow true north
with the river that first bore me

an organ laments

woe is i, the bright
perhaps brusque lining
onyx vessel of papercuts & piercings
buoyed forth in part by oils & osmosis
the envy of all elastic
every 27 days i dress anew
        7 years i renew all my stitching
my very fabric. how holy to cycle
with the moon & menses
to be rebirthed at the luckiest number of all
why do you dye me beige in the bath
                stain me bleach in the sink
who ordered you to go to war with me? erect
lavish memorials upon me. remember
when you still believed i was beautiful, when black
was your favorite color, when you were not afraid
of the dark

disordered food

listening to a thick amerikkkan accent is tiring, you
are trying to escape to the toilet only to find no bidet

strange. during your criminally—literally—short
break you run to buy some food. everything on

the menu is banned by the european union
so you bypass the court for the asian market

there is no pavement on your block
the nearest bus is ten blocks away
like the desert back home

post-op

sutures & futures shift
in the span of fourteen minutes
clip the tonsil, lacerate the adenoid
& all you will taste is red
the gum, the scab, the jelly
living on mute for days
is strange. what is heard in the quiet
drills on the roof of your mouth
sledgehammers the walls of your throat
the sour tinge of cauterized nerves
pendulums to frozen foods only. sleeptalk
on oxy & snitch on yourself
try to shake off the clenching
hallucinate in all six senses

split

thinning skin slipped between wet tissue
body at rest, mind always in motion
spirit restless, disorders always in limbo

my fears tattle on me but they are
the most honest parts of me
these fears walk big, talk tall
run deep & gently interrupt
my sleep. despite being water
i feel real at home in the earth
do my best work in the mud
the mundane, too, is a miracle

alternatives are endless but you can only be
somewhen, one somewhere at a time. the soft kills
are fresh. death & i talk mad shit when no one is listening

when you discover

a condom wrapper under his bed
the rusting tap is still dripping
& you towel off the last of your sleep
the bluing carpet is crisp, spotless. you bend
to lather your calves & catch
a crinkle under the bed
you pick out the gold foil easily
notice the spring flurries blurry by
& the calm of the breeze stills
you rigid. you examine the rip, mind the tear
slowly pull up the bar code
in an incognito window to confirm
trojan, magnum, raw
the ironies clog your throat

you grow hoarse
suffocate your gut & continue
moisturizing, grind the butter
& pocket the jagged wrapper for later
when you are fully dressed, you are resolved
the morning glides smoothly, he makes breakfast
divine, berry compote, tart as his humor
you catalog every facial shift & laugh
so breezily, he misses your one tell
his hands reach for you but you are still far away, stuck stupid
under his bed. it's your turn to choose so you play
your comfort film & he actually humors the plot
laughs even. did you know he had different laughs
you wonder how he laughs with

no. patience. keep cataloging, you are clinical to a fault, but it's the only
way to hold yourself as the stitches snap, quite unseemly you quietly pick
him apart turn over joke after joke, nothing is too small for your scrutiny
you silently grasp for a way to light him up without burning yourself
he drives you back to your studio, the conversation staccatos, the sun
squirms despite yourself, you choke, postpone your questioning
& instead brave a phone call right as he peels away. after he does
not kiss you at your doorstep. again you waste your last
mustard seed on him & his first reaction is laughter.
the usual falsehoods: i would never, i could not
imagine, i do not know how that got there
he even has the gall to stall & lengthen
the phone call after denying everything
three separate times. such are the delusions
of a man. he hates his father so much
that he becomes him. he finally breaks
things off, two weeks later. the gaslighting
piles in your lap as you painstakingly guide
him through ending things. things that he likes
but does not want. you, the thing unwanted

clench

how clumsy the fist
so biting the nerve
quite meaty the knuckle

unbuckle your excess
& draw near to your turgid heart
the four chambers wrenched ajar
so far, only bound by three fissures

then sever the tides that break
against our grief, our ever wandering grief
untie the fallopian in time
for the rainy season, birth all that you lost
in the drought

digest the dregs at the bottom
of a silvered cup & offer thanks
for small mercies, that will not quite seal
the fraying sinews
of your quartered
muscle

the moving portrait of the dying girl

they will say she lived the wonderful life
loved so loud & laughed so full
truly the envy of the town. is it not
so sad that she went so soon, so quiet
they will offer posthumous accolades
in honor of the moving, dying girl
they will host galas & fundraisers
create scholarships & fellowships
grant prizes & awards in her dead name
form committees & task forces
to make sure something like *this* never
happens again. they will immortalize her
say, she could have lived forever. they will
romanticize her. say, was she not
so lovely & how we all loved her
they will reduce her. to their guilt
& their shame & their insincere tears
oh, but think, just think, of how moving
the portrait of the dying girl will be

burning bushes

on the day the young soldier lights
himself on fire, i spot fireflies out
of season, outside the capital. such stark
contrasts even in their waning
daylights. they radiate
with an out-of-place brilliance
& then their lights dim
rather calmly. a slow fade
that brings me back
abruptly to the scene: a heavy dusk
with no way to preserve
my witnessing. only the echo
of a headline, the flick of a wick
the sparking of an ember

dust cloud

floaters

skyline striped by cirrus
tallest tales flipped on the highest of peaks
the oxygen mask is an afterthought
while turbulence tosses the conscious
to & fro. static abounds & wrappers
confound even the cleanest of sweeps
i am steeple, for a change. i think
it strange that i am not drunk on carbon
vapors. backseat makes concrete the finitude
of a vessel, the meat of our folly. so wholly
i am tugged back by grounding lighting
amused at the economy of attention
an aftershock of misfired pain signals
is my steadfast companion. with these
chatty neurons, there is only lonely. hazy
clockspun days. well, come by some time
linger in the chronic with me

gambit

the bloodied queen checks
her mate before squaring off
at the edging diagonal
callback to the pawn's
transformation
a power of its own making
stakes are pretty
high when you can move
every single piece at will

vegan

look, at me
playing, the greenest girl
with my plastic handbag
over my plastic dress
beneath my plastic trench coat
keeping my scales out of sight
swishing my plastic ponytail
behind my plastic eyelashes
with my plastic leggings
in my plastic go-go boots
to match my plastic gloves
keeping my claws out of sight
forgetting to leave a large plastic tip
with my plastic pencil
sheathed in my plastic pencil case
paint on a plastic smile
keeping my fangs out of sight
reminding myself of my plastic pills
in my plastic pill case
for my microplastic blood

gamma

unspined, left
at the right turn
yet we tweak it in
the wrong vein
intertwine just
on time in the same lane

try, in vain, to distinguish
heartbeat from heartbeat
bloodpump to bloodpump

sewing my patchwork lungs
back together as i sow
the threadbare bones back intact
there i are, beckoning
in all my multitudes, ones known
& ones yet unknown

consider the self

the agender, the gender-neutral, the genderfluid
that crucial prefix: wer- in place of wo-
how womanhood is predicated on wooing
just how tense "werman" sits on the tongue

consider the olde english
gender appropriation, according to a billionaire
being suffixed from hate to fear
from an -ism to a -phobia

consider the panic of gender
that hate & love are not opposites
the woman sounding human
our kind-ness, our very people-hood

scopes

virgo[2] go home
to your heart & lay
the lonely in the tub, wade through the red
from stellium to stellium & be buoyed
by the bubble of your gut. instinct tells us that we are a host
unto ourselves so we expand our definition of hospitality & lean in
to respectability politic. king
abandoned by queen is how i play the long game, always play a long
game. for almost anything at least once. in a lifetime
i encounter the ulcer, gas me up, the gall to believe i will know it all
someday. anyway, if men are from mars & women are from venus
then where does the cancer duo who flirts
beyond the binary land? far far away
dream of wind in my midheaven
the only air for light years
uncharted. lucille was born in babylon, but i moved here
when i was ten. so no surprises in my ascendance. left most of me
in the first house that followed. tough pills & shallow swallows come
aplenty but they will not harden me. made of mostly earth but
soft to the bone. skin thinned over time & shows no sign of stopping
save for my double cap
that covers my stubborn g a p

by & by

rusty eaves confetti me
as frostbitten stems pitter at my feet

in response to the call
regurgitate a litany for duality

call out my own name
plead for my own palms

bleed amber & be threaded bare
along the horse hair of a bow

leak pearl & be strung stiff
along refined clavicles & wired calves

high tides temper my tenderized cords
these so-called heartstrings

my chameleon heart trades spaces
with my chimerical brain, a multi-wanting organ

burgundy

here's a loveliness for you
polka dots pop lucky, says

my clairvoyant auntie & in turn
charm rouges my skin in full bloom

black will always be the new black
but all these spots make me faint

so when a ladybug kisses my wrist
on the last day of summer

i shed my penultimate tears
& laugh in changing colors

mental gymnastics

simone biles chooses herself
so i drop the balancing act
quit contorting in my skin, tight
stop jumping through blistering

h   o   o   p   s

& bending over backwards on cue
i do not weave ~~tightropes~~ anymore
my feet are reacquainted with rest
i do not miss the spiraling

t
r
a
p
e
z
e

& i let the juggling cease
the last echo of roaring
a p p l a u s e*
dies, finally pick up my own voice
a chorus of praise for my homecoming

game set match

racquets hung, but serena
& her majik will last her lifetimes
after all she is given divine blessings
training with venus herself even
the goddess of victory flew from paris
to anoint her lightning feet in saginaw
& she wears the hell out of those laurels

back talk stalks the champion of compton
working her quads hard for a quarter as much
such that she claps back against sneak attacks
kanekalon coils dance in glitter rainbow beads
that fuse into flawless diamonds for the final

hark, the superstar who sports every palette
reminiscent of the very first saint serena of rome
throws it back & she ain't sorry, twerking in tulle
shines even blacker, the whiter they try to wash her
burns every asinine statistic spat at her obsidian skin
conjures belief in self when no one offers safe harbor
tucks her heart in the thickest skin, little olympia in hand
graces her court finale at 40—love, hard won, in every swing

surprisingly

my only experience with love
at first sight, was new york in june

the best poetry in the city lingers
on weathered benches of central park

waltz in the still blues & petals
you will see exactly what i mean

gawk at the hawkers & listen close
bridges yawn, alleys sigh in reply

pivot seamlessly between the grooves
of pidgin & patois & creole

the fire escapes above me while cabbies
talk & tax in time to greening pennies

locals go borough this, borough that
but it is the water that floods my heart

kale

can it be just us
kakazi, of course it can
consider me morose that it
is still a question to you
when i answered it long ago

can it just be us
kawala, it already is
the table is set for two
an incandescent heart
our laughter & tears

can it just be us
kakyala, it definitely will
let us share a pair of footprints
offer our kinship to the snow
mark the world for the free

can it just be us
kaishki, for you? always
carving time & holding space
for you is easy breathing
this bright & early

proto
star

emparadise

my satisfaction is glacial

a slow trudge with consistent scenery

taut muscle s t r a i n i n g towards an endless periphery

then suddenly

p
r
e
c
i
p
i
c
e

suddenly an avalanche of ecstasy

oh, completion

waiting will be the death of me

but until then, i m e l t

in sweet sweet agony

turning

morning filters through the dusty blinds
& dances on the fluffed pillows
floats to the tune of my running mind
juxtaposed with your skipping heartbeat
you, deep asleep, me, wide awake
wrapped around you wrapped around me
with nothing to do but stare
at your stunning resting face
God, even in sleep you are transparent
seasons are ever changing
& i do not know how much time
to steal in this moment of stillness
so i focus my energy, begin
scanning furiously, committing
every curve, every line, every freckle
to memory. note the color palette
bronze stubble, silver lining, gold lashes
you frown & i catalog how your face shifts
every crease, every bend, every last detail
of your evanescent face

euphoric

the way you just lay there
expectant
draped in promise
languid
a calm waiting
the blue light tracing your ankles
dancing all the way up
cut teeth tossed aside
hair soft
lips supple
gleaming in the bluer light
hands crossed just so
eyes searing as ever
sometimes fire
this time opal
how does one
even begin

flashes

you have me pinned
right to the spot
where we first kissed
you have me stuck
right on the floor
where we first danced
you have me transfixed
right at the moment
where we first rose
high on love

unwinding

you weave your fingers
in & out
rough then gentle
soft then hard
i weave my fingers
up & down
tight then loose
slow then fast
we weave our fingers together
open then closed
bound by so much more
than anyone can touch

push & pull

lovers splayed where lovers meet
basking in the crowning of a star
on the brink of a new sky
letting the wind mellow the burn
caress the sting, embrace the scar

lovers splayed where lovers sleep
drinking in the intimacy of bloom
on the cusp of a new birth
letting the words whittle the feeling
chip the sensation, carve the emotion

incept

a daylight series of dreams plays
with my realities. part one: i feel you
under my tongue, twist into the sheets
& am struck by your hazy beauty. we stretch
towards one another, click perfectly
in place, smile into the other's
hair. your timbre radiates through me but i clock
an inconsistency. i shake myself awake, into
the next dream. part two: i twist playfully
into the sheets, grazed by your fire
opal eyes. we grasp at each other, roll seamlessly
into place, sigh into the other's smile. your warmth
burns through me but, again, i sense
an inconsistency. i shake awake, into the next
dream. part three: i am struck by your open face. we lunge
for each other, lock instantly into place, inhale the other's
pulse. your soul holds mine, but i am weighted
once more, by the inconsistency. i shake the sleep
altogether, back into reality. a gulf, me staring breathless
at you, long out of conscious reach, still
fast asleep, on the other side
of the expanding bed

delilah lets go

come back to bed, you whisper, already
half-soaked in dreams. the shears lie
on the windowsill, wink playfully in the night's
light. i kiss your freckles & respond
with a promise, later

the candelabra raises an eyebrow as i turn
a corner. consider my choices
even we, exotic women, are tempted
by the wind. before the lure of duty can blind me, i blow
out the quartet. stew in the moonless midnight

i want to be strong for you, stronger than you
will ever be. maybe i can lose
the early hours of day lying
with you, not to you. perhaps
your lifelong curls should remain

so, the twenty silver pieces are returned
to the doorstep. i peel the burden off my fingers
run, aching, to you & burrow
in your arms. you startle, only half-awake. kiss me
quiet & we cling through our morning

your eyes, exactly how i left them, singing
in this version, the judges forget about us
& the scripture does not mention us
not even once—exactly
as the songstress promises

even/in

the birds gossip as you teeter
on the edge plunge your lunge in steeped
waters dive hard & carve deep your organ's fill
sip the noon sun & soak in the dunes
rake your hands through the tight coils of me
tease out the last of my thinning skin
scratch me wide awake
remain, remain, remain

dream us a little longer
whisper me peace & i will wrap you asleep
render me joy & i will drown you elation
baptize me love & i will bury you in my heart

forever will never be ours but for now we are
each other's paradise hidden
set aside to please the naked ear
an end of a world is near
a pink dawn is a promise
you drift a while longer in me
we spite the current
nowhere to rush no need to be
we simply are—the bees agree

profiling

watching him at the study is a marvelous unveiling
his curious smile just hanging there, doing God's work
right hand types as the left hand tugs his five o'clock shadow

wistful eyelashes strain to kiss lounging curls at his temple
long lines & deep creases be damned
a plain fan oversees the nook as a strong lamp

thrusts him into the spotlight. his lips make up
new mnemonics as his ochre eyes memorize
freckles splash everywhere, fingers thrum

coins toss, turn at his every stretch
the chair squeaks in unison for his tap dance
distant traffic hums in agreement. twice

he breaks the trance to remind me
that he loves me. thrice, i laugh in bliss

sensate

scared i am losing my scent
ask him what if i become anosmatic
what if i could not smell his wrist by morning
he does not waver
    tells me i can always listen to his palms
scared i am losing my ear
ask him what if i become deaf
what if i could not hear him laugh at dawn
he does not stutter
    tells me i can always hear him on my lips
scared i am losing my voice
ask him what if i become mute
what if i could not say i love you at noon
he does not linger
    tells me i can always say it with my eyes
scared i am losing my sight
ask him what if i become blind
what if i could not hold him in my gaze at dusk
he does not falter
    tells me i can always hold him in my arms
scared i am losing my touch
ask him what if i become numb
what if i could not feel him by night
he does not flounder
    tells me i always feel him in my heart

almonds & peaches

laid threadbare just for you
pruned around your heart
an organ woven by amygdala
high on the sweet essence
of your crest. bless you
by the day worship
you by night
might try to halt
salt shaky as i stop the clock
turning for another morning in
your heart. apart from our holy
i am only for you
crushed decadence & folly
we sway outside time & rime
transcendent. dependent
on the buoyancy of voice
but never ruminate too
long on our choice

spilling my guts

& following the entrails lead me back to you
sorting through the majik of a past
that tenses my body does not cut the cord
of three strands—woven to you
adoration for the loose curls kissing
your freckles. ululations for the sparks
flying through your eyes. praise for the
chaotic joy of night. gratitude for the still
happy of morning. torn from your side by pit
in my stomach, only to be brushed awake
from the dream. seems you lavish me
better than i do, oh the pull as you push
the edge out of my reach & draw
me into your arms—taut
awed by the steady in my haze
the grip softens to touch the breath. in case
this is the last one but as if it is the first

sickly sweet

i offer you hydrogen
peroxide kisses
& you, hungrily, receive them
my mouth, an open wound tinted
coral, yet unbleached by a raw sun.
my cheeks are too old to cherub, but they are
waxing nonetheless
cratered to perfection
each pit is lined with silver. my gums
a neapolitan dream, a rink
for your agile tongue
you figure eight the ulcers, tenderize the rims
my lips twitch in time with my hips
& punctuate every gasp for air

engrave

cleverly, you stroke me turquoise
as
i
rise
from
my
slumber
bathed in the spring of amnesia
now
i
set
sail
upon
the
flights of my fancy & breathe you deep
elated
i
stroke
the
cleverness
of
your
pose
as
you
turquoise my dusk, soaked in the fall of aphrodesia

our

    life
we come & we go
so you say, any way
i tell you i want a beautiful death
you offer me a soft one in lieu of a surprise
the brief terror of losing you bites
down, twice a day
once in the parking lot & again
after midnight
catatonic, i blink, let our temporal sink
in, the ritual tear slips past eyelash
you blink back & gesture me closer
hold me gently against stained lungs
in 3/3 time
a cadence beyond time
my very own metronome
pretty beats per minute
happy-go-lucky me
with you, my beloved
anomaly

intrinsicly

i crave you, you say, in every way
that one can without consuming me instantly, engulfing me whole
never knew there are so many ways to say, perfect
which really should qualify a special entrance just for your tongue
twisting deliciously through every crevice on this body
how fully you fill me, yet i awake, hungry
needing every reminder of how it feels to be tasted by you
drinking your last drops as your breath pools above me
our limbs spin a marvelous symphony, a cadence raw
some intangible motion we stop trying to put our fingers on
your scent is indelible, strewn in all things keratin
hair, nails & dead skin cells grace every sheet
whispers crescendo to perfect pitch & bow to the coda
grinding you still until we both have nothing left to give

makefast

four thousand nine hundred light years away from our planet
glowing in a northern corner of our galaxy on the wing of a swan

there dances a solar system shared by two suns tucked
away in a cross constellation as they graze each other

every seven days before gliding away until the next eclipse
which is to say, if i could hold you for eternity, once

a week, i would starburst today & burn for a billion more
tomorrows with you. taking turns being the brightest star as

we haul ass in a nebula big enough for two. make you beam laughing
gas as we unravel ancient humor & embrace the entropy of it all

Acknowledgments

Grateful to our one & only sun.

Grateful to all the waters & all the streets that shaped me.

Grateful to God, to my partner, to my siblings, to my best friends, to my close friends. You are, for me, a reflection of the Divine.

Grateful to my foremothers, Alison & Amelia, Joy & Joyce, Edna & Suza, to every ancestor whose blood, sweat, tears softened the path for me.

Grateful to my language teachers, literature teachers, undergraduate professors & graduate professors, especially Tracie & Elizabeth.

Grateful to my agent, my editor & my whole publishing team. Your commitment to my work continues to change my life.

Grateful to the editors of the *Brink Literary Magazine*, *Prompt Press*, *FEMS Anthology*, *20.35 Africa* anthology, *Sonora Review*, *Equatorial Magazine*,

Smartish Pace; who all published earlier versions of several poems tucked in this book.

Grateful to the Richard E. Guthrie Memorial Fellowship and the Iowa Writers' Workshop for all their financial support of my writing; this book began as my master's thesis.

Grateful to all the unknown & unnamed beings who loved me out of the lows, who loved me into the highs, who loved this book into existence.

Grateful to you, of course, dear reader & dear listener. Your time & your space are a precious gift to me.

About the Author

Tramaine Suubi is a multilingual writer from Kampala & a graduate of the Iowa Writers' Workshop.